Coagulations:
New
and
Selected
Poems

Author's List of Publications

Volumes of Poetry

Firespitter, New York: Bola Press, 1982.
Merveilleux Coup de Foudre Poetry of Jayne Cortez & Ted Joans, France: Handshake Editions, 1982.
Mouth on Paper, New York: Bola Press, 1977.
Scarifications, New York: Bola Press, 1973.
Festivals & Funerals, New York: Bola Press, 1971.
Pisstained Stairs and the Monkey Man's Wares, New York: Phrase Text, 1969.

Recordings

There It Is, New York: Bola Press, 1982.
Unsubmissive Blues, New York: Bola Press, 1980.
Celebrations and Solitudes, New York: Strata East Records, 1975.

Record Anthologies

Poets Read Their Contemporary Poetry, New York: Folkways Records, 1980, Album FL 9702
Life Is a Killer, New York: Giorno Poetry Systems Records, 1982.

Coagulations: New and Selected Poems

Jayne Cortez

Thunder's Mouth Press   New York   Chicago

Published in the United States by Thunder's
Mouth Press,
Box 780, New York NY 10025
and Box 11223, Chicago, IL 60611

Design by Linda Lake
Drawings by Mel Edwards

Funded in part by grants from the N.Y. State
Council on the Arts and the National Endow-
ment for the Arts.

Library of Congress Cataloging in
Publication Data
Cortez, Jayne.
Coagulations: new and selected poems.

I. Title.
PS3553.072C6   1984   811'.54   83-24180
ISBN 0-938410-21-0
ISBN 0-938410-20-2 (pbk.)

Distributed by
Persea Books
225 Lafayette St.
New York NY 10012
(212) 431-5270

Contents

Scarifications

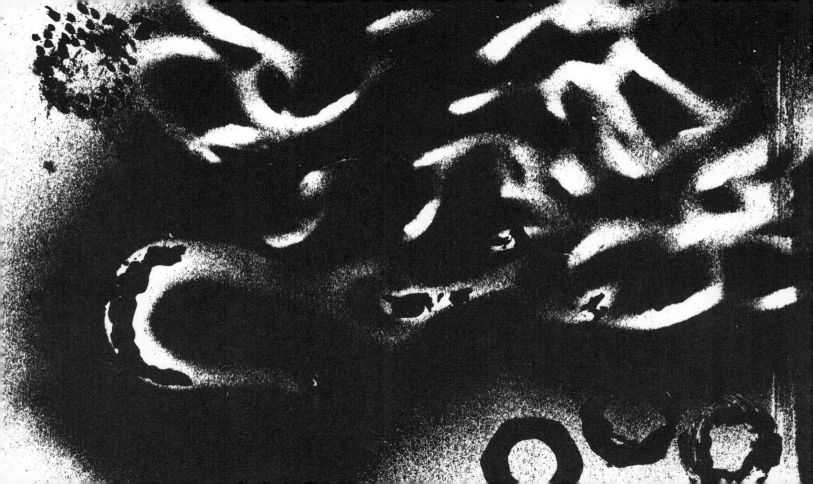

I Am New York City

i am new york city
here is my brain of hot sauce
my tobacco teeth my
mattress of bedbug tongue
legs apart   hand on chin
war on the roof   insults
pointed fingers   pushcarts
my contraceptives all

look at my pelvis blushing

i am new york city of blood
police and fried pies
i rub my docks red with grenadine
and jelly madness in a flow of tokay
my huge skull of pigeons
my seance of peeping toms
my plaited ovaries excuse me
this is my grime my thigh of
steelspoons and toothpicks
   i imitate no one

i am new york city
of the brown spit and soft tomatoes
give me my confetti of flesh
   my marquee of false nipples
my sideshow of open beaks
   in my nose of soot
in my ox bled eyes
in my ear of saturday night specials

   i eat ha ha hee hee and ho ho

i am new york city
never change never sleep never melt
my shoes are incognito
cadavers grow from my goatee
look i sparkle with shit with wishbones
my nickname is glue-me

take my face of stink bombs
my star spangled banner of hot dogs
take my beer can junta
my reptilian ass of footprints
and approach me through life
approach me through death
approach me through my widow's peak
through my split ends my
asthmatic laugh   approach me
through my wash rag
half ankle   half elbow
massage me with your camphor tears
salute the patina and concrete
of my rat tail wig
face up   face down   piss
into the bite of our handshake

i am new york city
my skillet-head friend
my fat-bellied comrade
citizens
break wind with me

Consultation

I have lived in circles of solitude
in support of my involved laughter
emerging from words
from an atmosphere of folded hands
and the half lip stroke of burnt respect
becoming noble while pounding an old love bone
in withered consultation
and without warning
i wiggle through dead hairs of dead gods
no change in volume
i too can be pain in the face of your body
speak to me about this confinement
this deep revelation
between pauses
and the earth fonk of discharge
pearl tongue submissions of enslaved tears
manhood   womanhood   childhood
the zigzag message from my teeth
heard by my lips
bold against painted spirits
of hunchback fear
   (as if i couldn't fly away from this road show of
      passing syringes)
No
it is the convulsion of limbs lying
in pose of a person
empty of all confidence
that will make the ritual invasion of death
spread like grease
through scalps of decorative hairdos

Do You Think

Do you think this is a sad day
a sad night
full of tequila   full of el dorado
full of banana solitudes

And my chorizo face a holiday for knives
and my arching lips   a savannah for cuchifritos
and my spit curls a symbol for you
to overcharge   overbill   oversell me
these saints   these candles
these dented cars   loud pipes
no insurance and no place to park
because my last name is Cortez

Do you think this is a sad night
a sad day

And on this elevator
between my rubber shoes
in the creme de menthe of my youth
the silver tooth of my age
the gullah speech of my one trembling tit
full of tequila   full of el dorado
full of banana solitudes you tell me
i use more lights   more gas
more telephones   more sequins   more feathers
more iridescent headstones
you think i accept this pentecostal church
in exchange for the lands you stole

And because my name is Cortez
do you think this is a revision

of flesh studded with rivets
  my wardrobe clean
the pick in my hair
  the pomegranate in my hand
14th street delancey street 103rd street
  reservation where i lay my skull
the barrio of need
  the police state in ashes
drums full of tequila full of el dorado
  full of banana solitudes say:

Do you really think time speaks english
  in the men's room

Bowery Street

new york

won't you confess

your private affairs

inside booth ears

of a leather uterus

who cares about the bumps on your tongue

cup of spit listen

i was bending against the railing

when i saw

go down shadow of your thing

and thanks to corn meal

i tell you this

not in falsetto

not in swine posture

but in my devotion to snot

we resemble

Feathers

Excite my breasts

and patrol my vagrant heart

bloodshot tongue of veins

today stands

the wet kiss liver of passion

against charcoal gums of my soul's teeth

Oh the fatness of love

(compared to tumors fly away my friends)

these scabs have taken eyes

and navels have taken off shades

to look experience in its nose

bartender of bars

a drink to the length of that

dog called loneliness

the sparrow mouth ruby

dry feathers on my lover's step

Lynch Fragment 2
(Autumn in New York, 72)

I am bleed mouth nod
from an oath in sorrow

i command both rise and fall
through melancholy links
of refugee sweat

i succulent republic of swamp lips
push forward my head through
windshields of violence
to baptise in a typhoon of night sticks

Scream on me

i've gasolined my belly against suspects
and flown away tears across
the dry rust wings of a roach god

Attention all units

i call to the fumes
drawn back against steel
against invisible fuck of a cry
to remove its road block flesh of a flunky
and let that rotting become feast
on sapphire of my adobe fangs

i am zest from bad jaw quiver
of aftermath

Come Celebrate Me

Tapping
(for Baby Laurence, and other tap dancers)

When i pat this floor
    with my tap

when i slide on air
and fill this horn intimate with
the rhythm of my two drums

   when i cross   kick
scissor locomotive

  take four for nothing
four we're gone

when the solidarity of my yoruba turns
join these vibrato feet
  in a Johnny Hodges lick
a chorus of insistent Charlie Parker riffs

  when i stretch out for a chromatic split
together with my double X
  converging in a quartet of circles

when i dance my spine in a slouch
slur my lyrics with a heel slide
arch these insteps in free time

  when i drop my knees
when i fold my hands
  when i decorate this atmosphere
with a Lester Young leap and

enclose my hip like snake repetitions
in a chanting proverb
    of the freeze

I'm gonna spotlite my boogie
    in a Coltrane yelp

echo my push in a Coleman Hawkins whine

i'm gonna frog my hunch in a Duke Ellington strut

quarter stroke my rattle
    like an Albert Ayler cry

i'm gonna accent my march in a Satchmo pitch

    triple my grind in a Ma Rainey blues

i'm gonna steal no steps

i'm gonna pay my dues

i'm gonna 1 2   3

    and let the people in the apple
go hmmmp   hmmmmp   hmmmmmp

It's Nothing

It's nothing

this tragedy in our arms

we can invent new bones

new flesh

new flowers against madness

another red dress

another applejack

another mug from

the neck bend of our conflict

yes

we can tolerate a still heart

against our ears and

relax with the crusted

confessions of a blood cake

it's nothing

Mouth on Paper

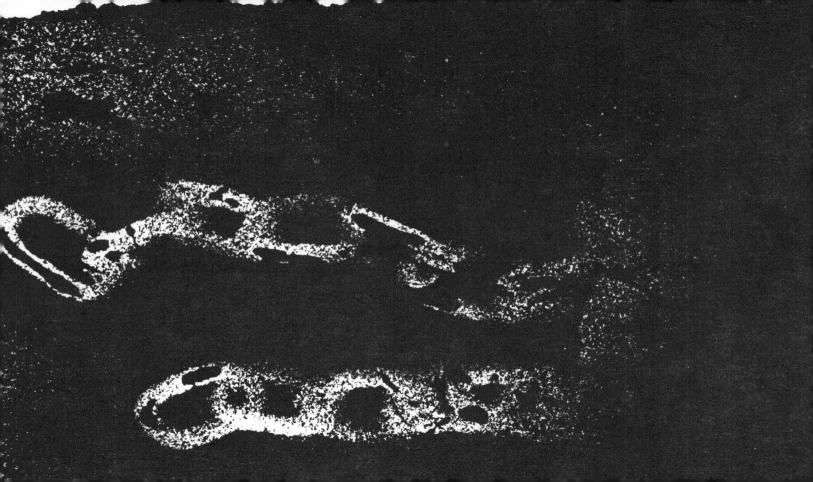

For the Poets
(Christopher Okigbo & Henry Dumas)

I need kai kai   ah
a glass of akpetesie   ah
from torn arm of Bessie Smith   ah

I need the smell of Nsukka   ah
the body sweat of a durbar   ah
five tap dancers   ah
and those fleshy blues kingdoms from deep south   ah
to belly-roll forward praise
for Christopher Okigbo   ah

I need a canefield of superstitious women   a
fumes and feathers from port of Lobito   a
skull of a mercenary   a
ashes from a Texas lynching   a
the midnight snakes of Damballah   a
liquid from the eyeballs of a leopard   a
sweet oil from the ears of an elder   a
to make a delta praise for the poets   a

On this day approaching me like a mystic
number   oh
in this time slot on death row   oh
in this flesh picking Sahelian zone   oh
in this dynamite dust and dragon blood and liver
cut   oh

I need cockroaches   ah
congo square   ah
a can of skokian   ah
from flaming mouth of a howling wolf   ah

I need the smell of Harlem ah
spirits from the birthplace of Basuto ah
mysteries from an Arkansas pyramid ah
shark teeth ah
buffalo ah
guerrillas in the rainy season ah
to boogie forward ju ju praise for Henry Dumas ah

In this day of one hundred surging zanzi bars oh
In this day of bongo clubs moon cafes and paradise
lounges oh
In this day's pounded torso of burgundy mush oh
In this steel cube in this domino in this dry
period oh

I need tongues like coiling pythons ah
spearheads gushing from gulf of Guinea ah
the broken ankles of a B.J. Vorster ah
to light up this red velvet jungle ah
i need pink spots from the lips of trumpet
players ah
the abdominal scars of seven head hunters ah
a gunslit for electric watermelon seeds ah
to flash a delta praise for the poets ah

Because they'll try and shoot us
like they shot Henry Dumas huh
because we massacre each other
and Christopher Okigbo is dead uh-huh
because i can't make the best of it uh-hun
because i'm not a bystander uh-hun
because mugging is not my profession uh-unh

I need one more piss-ass night to make a
hurricane a
i need one more hate mouth racist

sucking the other end of another gas pipe to make
flames   a
i need one more good funky blood pact
to shake forward a delta praise for the poets   a

On this day of living dead Dumas
on this day of living dead Okigbo

I need kai kai   ah   i need durbars   ah   i need torn
arms   ah
i need canefields   ah   i need feathers   ah   i need
skulls   ah
i need ashes   ah   i need snakes   ah   i need
eyeballs   ah
i need cockroaches   ah   i need sharkteeth   ah   i
need buffalo   ah
i need spirits   ah   i need ankles   ah   i need
hurricanes   ah
i need gas pipes   ah   i need blood pacts   ah   i
need   ah
to make a delta praise for the poets   ah

Brooding

They're brooding in Rosedale
with pipe-bombs in their mouths

Brooding in Boston
with darts between their teeth

Brooding in Connecticut
with curses on their tongues

Brooding with the smell of rat's piss in their hearts
brooding with the breath of red whisky in their spit
brooding into madness into death into sheets
   drying up
   while brooding brooding brooding brooding
brooding

These bloodthirsty people

They're brooding in North Dakota with grenades in
their hands
brooding in the Carolinas with torches in their ears
brooding in Alabama with water hoses still under
their hoods
brooding in Louisville with gasoline in their beer cans

Brooding in New York City with long nails shooting
from their hockey sticks
brooding in Puerto Rico with sterilization on their
minds
brooding in South Africa with cactus missiles perched
on their thighs
just brooding brooding brooding brooding brooding

They're brooding with purple veins of the bible
shooting from their noses
brooding with brass knuckles on their toes
brooding with badges under their chins
brooding with bricks in their baby carriages
brooding with prayers in their belts
just brooding brooding brooding brooding brooding

They're brooding with stiff upper lips for brooding
they're brooding with rules for brooding
they're brooding with heli-cannons for brooding
they're brooding with hate in their eyes for brooding
they're brooding with withered wreaths on their
heads for brooding
they're burning books while brooding
burning buses while brooding
throwing stones while brooding

These bloodthirsty people

They're brooding beyond the deadline
for brooding brooding brooding brooding

In the Morning

Disguised in my mouth as a swampland
nailed to my teeth like a rising sun
you come out in the middle of fish-scales
you bleed into gourds wrapped with red ants
you syncopate the air with lungs like screams from
yazoo
like X rated tongues
and nickel plated fingers of a raw ghost man
you touch brown nipples into knives
and somewhere stripped like a whirlwind
stripped for the shrine room
you sing to me through the side face of a black
rooster

In the morning   in the morning   in the morning
all over my door like a rooster
in the morning   in the morning   in the morning

And studded in my kidneys like perforated hiccups
inflamed in my ribs like three hoops of thunder
through a screw
a star-bent-bolt of quivering colons
you breathe into veiled rays and scented ice holes
you fire the space like a flair of embalmed pigeons
and palpitate with the worms and venom and wailing
flanks
and somewhere inside this fever
inside my patinaed pubic and camouflaged slit
stooped forward on fangs
in rear of your face
you shake to me in the full crown of a black rooster

In the morning   in the morning   in the morning

Masquerading in my horn like a river
eclipsed to these infantries of dentures of diving
spears
you enter broken mirrors through fragmented pipe
spit
you pull into a shadow ring of magic jelly
you wear the sacrificial blood of nightfall
you lift the ceiling with my tropical slush dance
you slide and tremble with the reputation of an
earthquake

and when i kick through walls
to shine like silver
when i shine like brass through crust in a compound
when i shine   shine   shine
you wail to me in the drum call of a black rooster

In the morning   in the morning   in the morning
gonna kill me a rooster
in the morning
early in the morning
way down in the morning
before the sun passes by
in the morning   in the morning   in the morning

In the morning
when the deep sea goes through a dog's bite
and you spit on tip of your long knife

In the morning   in the morning
when peroxide falls on a bed of broken glass
and the sun rises like a polyester ball of menses
in the morning

gonna firedance in the petro
in the morning
turn loose the blues in the funky jungle
in the morning
I said when you see the morning coming like
a two-headed twister
let it blow   let it blow
in the morning   in the morning
all swollen up like an ocean in the morning
early in the morning
before the cream dries in the bushes
in the morning
when you hear the rooster cry
cry rooster cry
in the morning   in the morning   in the morning

I said
disguised in my mouth as a swampland
nailed to my teeth like a rising sun
you come out in the middle of fish-scales
you bleed into gourds wrapped with red ants
you syncopate the air with lungs like screams from
yazoo
like X rated tongues
and nickel plated fingers of a raw ghost man
you touch brown nipples into knives
and somewhere stripped like a whirlwind
stripped for the shrine room
you sing to me through the side face of a black
rooster

In the morning   in the morning   in the morning

Give Me the Red on the Black of the Bullet
(For Claude Reece Jr.)

Bring back the life
of Claude Reece Jr.

I want the bullet from his head
to make a Benin bronze
to make an explosion of thunder
to make a cyclone

I want the 14 years of Claude Reece Jr.
shot on the 15th day of september
shot in the back of his head
shot by a police officer
shot for being black

Give me the black on the red of the bullet
i want to make a tornado
to make an earthquake
to make a fleet of stilts
for the blackness of Claude Reece Jr.
the blackness called dangerous weapon
called resisting an arrest
called nigger threat

I want the life of the blackness of Claude Reece Jr.
i want the bullet from his head
to make a protective staff for startled children
to make hooks and studs
for warrior masks

Give me the bullet with the odor
and the smoke and the skin and
the hair of Claude Reece Jr.
i want to make power
to make power
for the blackness of Claude Reece Jr.
the blackness called pent-up frustration
called unidentified negro
called nigger revolutionary

I want the life of the blackness of Claude Reece Jr.
i want the bullet from his head
to make a protective staff for startled children
to make a Benin bronze
to make an explosion of thunder
to make a cyclone
i want the bullet to bring back the blood
of Claude Reece Jr.
i want to make justice

I want to make justice for
the blackness of Claude Reece Jr.
bring back the bullet with the blood of the blackness
of Claude Reece Jr.
i want to make justice
i want to make justice
i want to make justice for the blackness
of Claude Reece Jr.

So Many Feathers

You danced a magnetic dance
in your rhinestones and satin banana G-strings
it was you who cut the river
with your pink diamond tongue
did the limbo on your back
straight from the history of southern flames
onto the stage where your body
covered in metallic flint
under black and green feathers strutted
with wings of a vulture paradise on your head
strutted among the birds
until you became terror woman of all feathers
of such terrible beauty
of such fire
such flames
all feathers Josephine
This Josephine
exploding red marble eyes in new york
this Josephine
breaking color bars in miami
this Josephine
mother of orphans
legion of honor
rosette of resistance
this Josephine before
splitting the solidarity of her beautiful feathers

Feather-woman of terror
such feathers so beautiful
Josephine
with your frosted mouth half-open
why split your flamingos

with the death white boers in durban south africa
Woman with magnificent face of Ife mask
why all the teeth for the death white boers in durban
Josephine you had every eyelash in the forest
every feather flying
why give your beaded snake-hips
to the death white boers in durban
Josephine didn't you know about the torture
chambers
made of black flesh and feathers
made by the death white boers in durban
Josephine terror-woman of terrible beauty of such
feathers
I want to understand why dance
the dance of the honorary white
for the death white boers in durban

After all Josephine
I saw you in your turquoise headdress
with royal blue sequins pasted on your lips
your fantastic legs studded with emeralds
as you kicked   as you bumped   as you leaped in the
air
then froze
your body breaking lightning in fish net
and Josephine   Josephine
what a night in harlem
what electricity
such trembling
such goose pimples
so many feathers
Josephine
dancer of the magnetic dancers
of the orange flint pelvis of the ruby navel
of the purple throat

of the feet pointing both ways
of feathers now gone
Josephine   Josephine
I remember you rosette of resistance
southern flames
Josephine of the birdheads, ostrich plumes
bananas and sparkling G-strings
Josephine of the double-jointed knees
double-jointed shoulders   double-jointed thighs
double-jointed breasts   double-jointed fingers
double-jointed toes   double-jointed eyeballs
double-jointed hips doubling
into a double squat like a double star into a giant
double snake
with the double heartbeats of a young girl
doubling into woman-hood
and grinding into an emulsified double spirit
Josephine terror-woman of feathers   i remember
Josephine of such conflicts   i remember
Josephine of such floating   i remember
Josephine of such heights   i remember
Josephine
of so many transformations   i remember
Josephine
of such beauty   i remember
Josephine of such fire   i remember
Josephine of such sheen   i remember
Josephine
so many feathers   i remember
Josephine   Josephine

Rose Solitude
(For Duke Ellington)

I am essence of Rose Solitude
my cheeks are laced with cognac
my hips sealed with five satin nails
i carry dreams and romance of new fools and old
flames
between the musk of fat
and the side pocket of my mink tongue

Listen to champagne bubble from this solo

Essence of Rose Solitude
veteran from texas   tiger from chicago   that's me
i cover the shrine of Duke
who like Satchmo   like Nat (King) Cole
will never die because love they say
never dies

I tell you from stair steps of these navy blue nights
these metallic snakes
these flashing fish skins
and the melodious cry of Shango
surrounded by sorrow
by purple velvet tears
by cockhounds limping from crosses
from turtle skinned shoes
from diamond shaped skulls and canes
made from dead gazelles
wearing a face of wilting potato plants
of grey and black scissors
of bee bee shots and fifty red boils
yes the whole world loved him

I tell you from suspenders of two-timing dog odors
from inca frosted lips
nonchalant legs
i tell you from howling chant of sister Erzulie
and the exaggerated hearts of a hundred pretty
women
they loved him
this world sliding from a single flower
into a caravan of heads made into ten thousand
flowers

Ask me
Essence of Rose Solitude
chickadee from arkansas that's me
i sleep on cotton bones
cotton tails
and mellow myself in empty ballrooms
i'm no fly by night
look at my resume
i walk through the eyes of staring lizards
i throw my neck back to floorshow on bumping goat
skins
in front of my stage fright
i cover the hands of Duke who like Satchmo
like Nat (King) Cole will never die
because love they say
never dies

Nighttrains

When i blow open green bottles
straight across hump of a frozen tongue

when i shove brown glass
through skull of a possum
and pass from my ears a baptism of red piss

when i cry from my butt like a jackal
and throw limbs of a dying mule into the river

when i spit venom from the head
burn codeine into a cosmetic paste
and grieve into a wax of dried bulls

when my mystical bunions
like steel hearses jam eyes
into searching spit of a starving wolf
into cosmic lips like monkey genitals

And i receive my pickled turned skeleton of rusty
chains
in the bodega
i receive a symbolic heart made of five middle fingers
in the bodega
i receive a teeth parade of yellow roses to leave the
bodega
and cross the rio grande
onto the flat-bed bones of a musty nighttrain

I say
to see me loosen jaws like a snake
to see me exhausted after a few strikes

to see me pay dirt to the ice hog
in my masai-pachuca-doo
squatting on a pillow of old zoot suits
squatting among the names and breeds
breaking down cheeks dotted
on this night train
and i say i dream of the 1943 riots
I say i dream in a hail storm of riots
and i say riots dream into a mass of skins stooping
on flat bed bones of a funky nighttrain

And when i syphon sweat for fuel
from this patron saint of chronic diarrhea

When i turn this rubber face into a spotted puma
and take on the forceful winds of the prune pickers

When my laughter dominates the last seat
and i burn labor contracts into brown port caca

And then i approach in mother of pearl and human
blood
in father of smoking and coughing throats
in my jelly of coyote strings
who is to say what when i approach

I mean somewhere along the road in this cold cold
chicken shit
somewhere along the road in this wasted body
somewhere along the road eat stocks, bonds, feathers
somewhere along the road confiscate borders from
wild dogs
somewhere along the road shove them into the
imperial valley
somewhere along the road cry hard

and let this night train sink its
rundown rectum of electric chairs into heaven
and say fuck it

I see a way through the maroon glass of this milky
way
I say i see a way through for the cradle of hulls
sticking through these indigo ankles
I see a way through
for these torn shoes stinking like dead cats
I see a way through for these blood streaked legs
I say i see a way through
for these puss riddled holes in their suction cup lips
and when i pass through toothless combs coming
from armpits
of the bodega
when i pass through bats on corkscrews coming
from the bodega
when i push my mortified flesh from this bodega
and walk with the mildew of an old zoot suit
walk tall in my mud-packed-masai-pachuca-doo
walk among the survivors from the musty night trains
fuck it
I say dreams are like riots
I say we dream in a hailstorm of riots
and i say riots dream into a mass of skins
coming from flat-bed bones of the funky funky
nighttrains

You Know
(For the people who speak the you know language)

You know
   I sure would like to write a blues
you know
  a nice long blues
you know
   a good feeling piece to my writing hand
you know
   my hand that can bring two pieces of life
   together in your ear
you know
   one drop of blues turning a paper clip
   into three wings and a bone into a revolt
you know
   a blues passing up the stereotype symbols
you know
   go into the dark meat of a crocodile
   and pin point the process
you know
   into a solo a hundred times
   like the first line of Aretha Franklin
you know
   like Big Mama Thornton
you know
   i sure would like to write a blues
you know
   if i could write me a blues
you know
   a blues that you could all feel at the same time
   on the same level like a Joe Louis punch

you know
a punch that could break a computer
into an event like Guinea Bissau
you know
if i could write me a blues
you know
a nice long blues
you know
an up to the minute blues
you know
a smack dab in the middle of depression blues
you know
a blues without incidental music
you know
without spending time being incidental
you know
if i could write a blues
you know
a blues without the popular use of the word love
you know
without running love love love in the ground
you know
a serious blues
you know
a significant blues
you know
an unsubmissive blues
you know
a just because we exist blues
you know
a blues
you know
a terrible blues about the terrible terrible need
i have to write the blues

you know
   if i could write a nice long blues
you know
   a nice long blues
you know
   it sure would feel good to my writing hand
you know
   you know
   you know

For the Brave Young Students in Soweto

Soweto
when i hear your name
I think about you
like the fifth ward in Houston Texas
one roof of crushed oil drums on the other
two black hunters in buckets of blood
walking into the sweat and stink of Sharpeville
into the fire of Sharpeville
into your children's eyes suffering from malnutrition
while pellets of uranium are loaded onto boats
headed for France for Israel for Japan
away from the river so full of skulls
and Robben Island so swollen with warriors
and the townships that used to overflow
with such apathy and dreams
and i think about the old Mau Mau
grieving in beer halls
and the corrupt black leaders
singing into police whistles
and i think about the assembly line of dead
"Hottentots"
and the jugular veins of Allende
and once again how the coffin is divided into dry ink
how the factory moves like a white cane
like a volley of bullets in the head of Lumumba
and death is a death-life held together by shacks
by widows who cry with their nipples pulled out
by men who shake with electrodes on the tongue
and Soweto
when i hear your name and look at you on the
reservation
a Xhosa

44

in the humid wrinkles of Shreveport Louisiana
walking down fannin street
into the bottom hole in the wall of endurance
i smell the odor of our lives together made of tar
paper
the memories opening like stomachs in saw mills
the faces growing old in cigarette burns
and i think about the sacrifices made in Capetown
the sisters being mauled by police dogs
while the minister of justice rides
the tall ship of torture
down the hudson river in New York
while vigilantes under Zulu masks
strike through the heartland like robots
in military boots with hatchets made of apartheid lips
and Soweto
when i look at this ugliness
and see once again how we're divided and
forced into fighting each other
over a funky job in the sewers of Johannesburg
divided into labor camps
fighting over damaged meat and stale bread in
Harlem
divided into factions fighting to keep from fighting
the ferocious men who are shooting
into the heads of our small children

When i look at this ugliness
and think about the Native Americans pushed
into the famine of tribal reserves
think about the concentration camps full of sad
Palestinians
and the slave quarters still existing in Miami
the diamond factories still operating in Amsterdam in
Belgium

45

the gold market still functioning on wall street
and the scar tissues around our necks
swelling with tumors of dead leaves
our bodies exploding like whiskey bottles
as the land shrinks into the bones of ancestor
"Bushmen"
and i tell you Soweto
when i see you stand up in the middle of all this
stand up to the exotic white racists
in their armored churches
stand up to these landstealers, infant killers, rapists
and rats

to see you stand among the pangas the stones
the war clubs the armadillos dying along this roadside
to see you stand with the ocean the desert
the birthright of red cliffs
to see you stand with your brave young warriors
courageous and strong hearted
looking so confident in battle marks coated
in grief and gunmetal tears
to see you stand up to this epidemic of expansion
and flame passbooks into ashes
fling stones into the mouths of computers
to see you stand on the national bank of america
like monumental sculpture made of stained bullets
to see you stand empty handed
your shoulders open to the world
each day young blood falling on the earth
to see you stand in the armed struggle
next to Mozambique, Angola, Namibia, Zimbabwe
Soweto i tell you Soweto
when i see you standing up like this
i think about all the forces in the world
confronted by the terrifying rhythms of young
students

by their sacrifices
and the revelation that it won't be long now
before everything
in this world changes

Flame

And it's familiar
this fact of flame
of indulging images
the salty dust devil winds
spitting into silver helmets
through shit splattered wings
the beginnings and endings
in which i salute the sun
because i know it has to come today
because a dream is like a nail
because this room peels back the hole in my cup
and so i tell you whoever you are
plastic pen, paper, dictionary
                    i tell you
            the policemen sing
    the sanitation men whistle
the distended body of military parades
fly flags in wounds of dead words
and the sad look of tribal warfare
points every second between sockets
into the same flame of the zero hour
and i know it has to come from me

Firespitter

Firespitters
(FESTAC 77)

Firespitters
spitting across the desert
into feverdust rituals on Badagry road
a sanctified road full of ghostwriters
gin drinkers
lips spreading like
stripes and medals from the chest of my father
knife swallowers
wine tappers
torches gleaming like
the gold tooth of my mother
Firespitters
spitting across syncopating roaches into
sunsets falling like orange tams
on the heads of sweating soldiers
tangerine spit balls
going down into sewers of dark stout
a loud baritone night entering us between
pine streaked thighs of big city funk
a festival of firespitters in a mucus of brass bands
Lagos
in your beautiful nasty self shake everything
we're here
moving through the red fog like a giant defense plant
we open our boot tops and bones like nightsticks
throw
themselves into maneuvering shadows
we stand on the blunt wings of steel bees
a unit of bent fingers and torsos bending forward
like sharknives
we have jet propellered tongues

ten fifths of lightning
battle stars cholorophylled plungers horizonal jaws
painted skins swiveling pupils gut blasting moans and
the supersonic sound of invisible orchestras
sweet spirits of Nupe
listen to the Firespitters
a caravan of
Firespitters
spitting into the river of asbestos
into the trade wind of coral snakes
into marrows of guinea fowl
into a meridian of rice
one hundred and ninety spits in
a village libating like niagara falls
we drink this three thousand and seventy five proof
down-pour
spitting through chains of acrobatic fingers
in green caps
going up into the chalk eyed smell of wintertime
a slurring soprano dawn entering us
on outskirts of big city dumps
Lagos
dark puree of flesh in a mask of spinning mirrors
shake everything in your beautiful nasty self
we're here

The Red Pepper Poet
(For Leon Damas)

If you see a cycle of heavy breezes
blowing backward
into massive loops of heat
crossing two oceans after sunset
if you see an avalanche of clouds
pushing forward into jet streams with syncopated
thunder
before sunrise
if you see a long stroke of black lightning
flashing in the sky
like a fast flying train
on its way to Savannah at noontime
if you see a medley of slow moving currents
spinning into a hum of furious tornados
at midnight
Tell everybody
The Red Pepper Poet
moving like the eye of a hurricane is going home

Listen to the mud flow into its deep zydeco
the high speed drills in their tapping shoes
storm   flesh   flame
ethiopian ash rings
in this luminous hour of potassium bones
with wings like a magma of hot tears
flooding into mouth of the cayenne river

Listen to the shrill evening falsettos
and the filing down of teeth
hatchet dancers carving up shadows
knife men entering with lips of purple plated chrome

scar tissues opening their pigments
into the 21st century
Boom
Shoot off the guns for this elder
put your hair into the earth
and fill the night with fire ants
Go ahead
and show your respect for this freedom fighter
this great warrior
dangerous orphan
ibeji among ibeji
the Red Pepper Poet with the bull-roarer tongue
Go ahead
shoulder to shoulder
exile to exile
Dance for the Red Pepper Poet who fought so well
so long so many places so many times in
this world of so much suffering
Boni Boni Boni Boni

Won't you dance for this mean banjo player
this dignified volcano with his hat pushed to one side
and his eyebrow up
Won't you dance for the Red Pepper Poet with the
bull roarer tongue
Go ahead move into the flow of the deep zydecos
into the shrill evening falsettos and the grinding down
of teeth
Go ahead and decorate this ground with tobacco
leaves
with sea shells with broken bottles
with tiger balm cans with books with wooden
daggers
with dollheads with cornshuck
and a tall glass of scotch and soda

Go ahead and let the old time rhythms roll
for this great pain carrier poet
who carried his pain into the forest
like earth carries the amazon river
carried his pain
like a sizzling fever carries a hidden jungle
like the sea carries fish glue
and we carry the intensity of these
fragile vaporous magnetic words of revolt between
anthills of ice covered poverty
and fire coals burning next to iron spikes
on this day mixed in plantango weed
the smell of snake root
rain feathers
rusty nails in solitude of
a smoking typhoon drilling backward
in backwater lashes of hurricane sweat
triple time on stilts across a mardi gras mass
in angles   in circles   in green paste   in purple agua
Zoom

It's the agility of these popping veins
the strong knuckles of endurance
the expanding neck of unpublished flights
that we push together the amber oils up
split into drops one shake
dissect the meaning of the strategy of Damas
arriving on the concourse
the odor of rum and manioc in his hair
Strike up style spellbinder
You had it
and everybody loved the thickness of your accent
the ritual look of fierce crocodiles crossed in your
eyes
the secret memories and sacred visions knotted in

your smile
the indestructible timing of your spirit
and your natural slashing attitude
Red Pepper Poet with the bull-roarer tongue
Throw off the flames
flame thrower with your dark flesh barrel house band
come
and blow into our ears now blow

If you hear a solo wind
in sandpaper socks
sanding sounds of super heated stone songs
against sulphurous falling cells on
dry crust dogs
at the pulse of the hawk's scream
at the moment
when fifty drums hemorrhage
in the middle of the rhythms
when the hurricane turns
at the yoke of the curve
among dead spiders
at the end of the choice
when everything drops into your mask
in that position beyond all grief
at that second
this very instant
Won't you dance for the Red Pepper Poet
with the bull-roarer tongue
Go ahead
push your chair forward
and dance for the great warrior poet
who fought so well so long so many places
so many times in this world of so much suffering
Boni Boni Boni Boni

If the Drum is a Woman

If the drum is a woman
why are you pounding your drum into an insane
babble
why are you pistol whipping your drum at dawn
why are you shooting through the head of your drum
and making a drum tragedy of drums
if the drum is a woman
don't abuse your drum   don't abuse your drum
                        don't abuse your drum

I know the night is full of displaced persons
I see skins striped with flames
I know the ugly disposition of underpaid clerks
they constantly menstruate through the eyes
I know bitterness embedded in flesh
the itching alone can drive you crazy
I know that this is America
and chickens are coming home to roost
on the MX missile
But if the drum is a woman
why are you choking your drum
why are you raping your drum
why are you saying disrespectful things
to your mother drum your sister drum
your wife drum and your infant daughter drum
If the drum is a woman
then understand your drum
your drum is not docile
your drum is not invisible
your drum is not inferior to you
your drum is a woman
so don't reject your drum
don't try to dominate your drum

don't become weak and cold and desert your drum
don't be forced into the position
as an oppressor of drums
and make a drum tragedy of drums
if the drum is a woman
don't abuse your drum   don't abuse your drum
don't abuse your drum

Blood Suckers

In Miami
the blood suckers came sucking in full speed
twisting and sucking into
a urethra of decapitated shrimp heads
tongue slashing and sucking into
a matrix of turtle shells
rising up and sucking through
a perforated sac of southern crosses
drawing blood and resucking
the dried mutilated scalps of a Seminole nation
moaning and groaning and sucking on mucus from
nipples of tropical storm troopers
grunting and chewing and pissing on
the artificial hides
of stuffed alligators
Corrupted suckers dropping down and sucking
all the way through Brownsville to Coconut Grove
Blood Suckers
sucking on the joints of steel horses and trembling
sucking gopher meat from
the plastic womb of St. Mary on
the dixie highway and hallucinating
sucking on the moon over Miami
muck fire in the everglades sucked
Florida folks sunbathing on the swanee river sucked
telephoto lens sucked
deposits of uranium sucked
veins of manganese sucked
dry lizards jelly sucked
chrome   nickel   mercury   sucked
tax payers money sucked
A sucking extravaganza

in the brown coral coop of peruvian breasts
in the spanish moss wings of moorish armpits
tobacco ensemble fantasia
Blood Suckers
sucking slow motion sucks on the ends of
throbbing hoodoo spikes
sucking on the cracked heels of ancient bolito
winners
sucking through the rotten banana farts of
a jesuit priest
sucking through the contracting pupils of vicious
watch dogs
then fabricating sucks with
the Dupont suckers at the test sight
Blood Suckers
sucking on high powered rifle butts and splattered
glass
sucking on a column of smoking mickey mouse dolls
sucking on a sea sick refugee in the gulf stream
sucking on the panama canal treaty
sucking on sixty bars of gold
sucking on a thousand tons of rubble and
disfigurations
sucking at the Mr. Universe pageant
sucking with the firestone tire company executive
suckers
sucking with a security force of forced suckers
sucking with a conglomerate of born again christian
suckers
sucking with the general dynamic suckers of blood
suckers
Blood Suckers
sucking and sweating and hooting and balling
themselves
into knots on the red tide slime of Miami beach

A casino full of suckers turning tricks of justice and
vomiting into a palmetto of fluoridated snake ash
Addicted suckers
fucking and pecking and choking themselves to death
in
the weasel stink of little Pretoria
Blood Suckers
sucking with an asshole full of radioactive rust and
exploding way down in the dumps of Love Canal
expanding themselves and vigorously sucking on
a medley of birth defects
stealing land and sucking into
a grand jury of broken cow teeth
yelping and belching and collapsing in
the dark blue quick sand
of Liberty City
screaming and squabbling and wallowing and
suck suck suck suck sucking
all the way down in buzzard shit

Rape

What was Inez supposed to do for
the man who declared war on her body
the man who carved a combat zone between her
breasts
Was she supposed to lick crabs from his hairy ass
kiss every pimple on his butt
blow hot breath on his big toe
draw back the corners of her vagina and
hee haw like a California burro

This being war time for Inez
she stood facing the knife
the insults and
her own smell drying on the penis of
the man who raped her

She stood with a rifle in her hand
doing what a defense department will do in times of
war
And when the man started grunting and panting and
wobbling forward like
a giant hog
She pumped lead into his three hundred pounds of
shaking flesh
Sent it flying to the Virgin of Guadalupe
then celebrated day of the dead rapist punk
and just what the fuck else was she supposed to do?

And what was Joanne supposed to do for
the man who declared war on her life
Was she supposed to tongue his encrusted
toilet stool lips

suck the numbers off of his tin badge
choke on his clap trap balls
squeeze on his nub of rotten maggots and
sing god bless america thank you for fucking my life
away

This being wartime for Joanne
she did what a defense department will do in times of
war
and when the piss drinking shit sniffing guard said
I'm gonna make you wish you were dead black bitch
come here
Joanne came down with an ice pick in
the swat freak motherfucker's chest
yes in the fat neck of that racist policeman
Joanne did the dance of the ice picks and once again
from coast to coast
house to house
we celebrated day of the dead rapist punk
and just what the fuck else were we supposed to do

I See Chano Pozo

A very fine conga of sweat
a very fine stomp of the right foot
a very fine platform of sticks
a very fine tube of frictional groans
a very fine can of belligerent growls
a very fine hoop of cubano yells
very fine   very fine

Is there anyone finer today   olé   okay
Oye   I say
I see Chano Pozo
Chano Pozo from Havana Cuba   You're the one

You're the one who made Atamo into
a tattooed motivator of revolutionary spirits

You're the one who made Mpebi into
an activated slasher of lies

You're the one who made Donno into
an armpit of inflammable explosives

You're the one who made Obonu into
a circle of signifying snakes

You're the one who made Atumpan's head strike
against
   the head of a bird   everynight   everyday
in your crisscrossing chant
in your cross river mouth   You're the one

Oye   I say
Chano
what made you roar like a big brazos flood
what made you yodel like a migrating frog
what made you shake like atomic heat
what made you jell into a ritual pose
Chano   Chano   Chano
Chano   Chano
what made your technology of thumps so new so
mean
I say
is there anyone meaner than Chano Pozo
                              from Havana Cuba

Oye
I'm in the presence of ancestor
                              Chano Pozo

Chano connector of two worlds
You go and celebrate again with
the *compañeros* in Santiago
            and tell us about it
You go to the spirit house of Antonio Maceo
and tell us about it
You go to Angola
and tell us about it
You go to Calabar
and tell us about it
You go see the slave castles
you go see the massacres
you go see the afflictions
you go see the battlefields
you go see the warriors
you go as a healer
you go conjurate
you go mediate

you go to the cemetery of drums
return and tell us about it

Lucumi   Abakwá   Lucumi   Abakẃa

Olé   okay
Is there anyone finer today
Oye   I say
did you hear
Mpintintoa smoking in the palm of his hands
did you hear
Ilya Ilu booming through the cup of his clap
did you hear
Ntenga sanding on the rim of his rasp
did you hear
Siky Akkua stuttering like a goat sucking hawk
did you hear
Bata crying in a nago tongue
did you hear
Fontomfrom speaking through the skull of a dog
did you hear it   did you hear it   did you hear it

A very fine tree stump of drones
a very fine shuffle of shrines
a very fine turn of the head
a very fine tissue of skin
a very fine smack of the lips
a very fine pulse
a very fine *encuentro*
very fine   very fine   very fine
Is there anyone finer than
Chano Pozo from Havana Cuba
Oye   I say
I see Chano Pozo

There It Is

My friend
they don't care
if you're an individualist
a leftist   a rightist
a shithead or a snake

They will try to exploit you
absorb you   confine you
disconnect you   isolate you
or kill you

And you will disappear into your own rage
into your own insanity
into your own poverty
into a word a phrase a slogan a cartoon
and then ashes

The ruling class will tell you that
there is no ruling class
as they organize their liberal supporters into
white supremist lynch mobs
organize their children into
ku klux klan gangs
organize their police into
killer cops
organize their propaganda into
a device to ossify us with angel dust
pre-occupy us with western symbols in
african hair styles
innoculate us with hate
institutionalize us with ignorance
hypnotize us with a monotonous sound designed
to make us evade reality and stomp our lives away

And we are programmed to self destruct
to fragment
to get buried under covert intelligence operations of
unintelligent committees impulsed toward death
And there it is

The enemies polishing their penises between
oil wells at the pentagon
the bulldozers leaping into demolition dances
the old folks dying of starvation
the informers wearing out shoes looking for crumbs
the lifeblood of the earth almost dead in
the greedy mouth of imperialism
And my friend
they don't care
if you're an individualist
a leftist   a rightist
a shithead or a snake

They will spray you with
a virus of legionnaire's disease
fill your nostrils with
the swine flu of their arrogance
stuff your body into a tampon of
toxic shock syndrome
try to pump all the resources of the world
into their own veins
and fly off into the wild blue yonder to
pollute another planet

And if we don't fight
if we don't resist
if we don't organize and unify and
get the power to control our own lives
Then we will wear

the exaggerated look of captivity
the stylized look of submission
the bizzare look of suicide
the dehumanized look of fear
and the decomposed look of repression
forever and ever and ever
And there it is

No Simple Explanations
(To the memory of Larry Neal)

There are no simple explanations
not for the excesses
not for the accumulations
not for the lips of magnetic lava
not for the liver of explosive slits
not for the heart
          ready to shoot off like a volcano
There are no simple explanations

The altar will not fit another skull
and there are no more volunteers
no mixture of eyelashes and drops of blood
                    in the circle

no alliances drinking together
               in a night of dead events
no bulletproof faces in the air
no mask of erosion fermenting in slobber
no fetish trunk of sacrifices in disguise

Only the space of exasperation left by the advance
only juice from heat of its possession
the injunction of shadows
collectivity of ants
tongue of deified soot
flesh of incarcerated bones
but no simple explanations

Not for madness
reproducing itself through the uterus in the throat
not for sharks
having feeding frenzies in the middle of foreheads

not for
sentimental pass words of vomit splattering pages
No simple explanations

Let the index finger
    take responsibility
        for its smell
let the chickens protrude from drums
let the lagoon   the boat   the ancestors
    enter pores of a poet of pretty smiles

This piece is passing up the motif of sorrow
        let it pass
let the words split and erupt and dry
        into snake pulsations

Spit three times
    into ruby dust of your own snot
and paste it
    on callous of your self-conscious itch

I say lung   fire   of mouth-piece tremble
still warm and metal stone
conjuration and syntax
inverted stump under solitary root
                    of erratic falcons
weed of pain   of rupture   of panic
let it go down
        like body and soul
            in the horn of Coleman Hawkins
Sink into the insurrection of red shanks
into the high pitch voltage of mosquito hums
into liquified ankh of egyptian flames
sparrow house bubble of quiver
let your divination fall
        like body and soul
            in the horn of Coleman Hawkins

Ritual fart
and navel of rebellious stink
urination and energetic repulsion
poetic orgasm and gutteral belch of erotic storm
let your dynamism grunt

I say
make it shake forward like shimmering tumors of
okra stew
shake forward on a speckled canvas of menstrual
bandages
shake into sucking tubes of midnight flies
into the sub-dominant tilt of flinching eyeballs
into the intrinsic elasticity of violent impulses
Conform to evolution of your own syllables
to revolution of your own stanzas
because
suddenly it will be too soon
suddenly it will be too late
suddenly it will be too sudden
and there'll be no tuning forks left
in palm of a poet on a cold morning
no deposits of fat left
on neck of a blues at the crossroads
no spell of inspiration waiting
at foot of a cocaine pyramid
no ju ju leaves hidden
in the center of the whirlwind

Only abusive forces in absolute opposition to revolts
only burial grounds of radioactive mud
only bellies of unfinished poems
and time dismantling itself between invisible sticks
but no simple explanations

Not for the flesh of incarcerated bones
not for the tongue of deified soot
not for the womb of hoodoo hollerin' bebop ghosts

No simple explanations

Once Upon a Road

It was fun
traveling through the heart of this country
just what I needed
enough gasoline
to speed along the highway
in the winter morning
so crisp and white and dirty and cold
my poetry trying to escape the chill
but anyway
it was fun purging the heart of this country
wow
what a beer mug against
mug of a drunk lumberjack on
his way to South Africa
what electricity in mouth of a disco band so full
of the frenzy of nothing
what a great feeling to
look over shoulders of a liberty statue
look up into the oxidized head of
a country so pure in dumb bells
ding dong
what a crowd of Mr. and Mrs. Blank faces going off
to war
such a promotion of fear
such fleshless featherless balls
you make me laugh right in the middle of
this fucking poem
and that's not a device to get your attention
once upon a road
there was a country in the heart of
the Crow the Sioux and the Kickapoo

On All Fronts

Stockpiling

The stockpiling of frozen trees
    in the deep freeze of the earth
The stockpiling of dead animals
    in the exhaust pipes of supersonic rockets
The stockpiling of desiccated plants
    on the death root of an abcessed tooth
The stockpiling of defoliants
    in the pine forest of the skull
The stockpiling of aerosols
    in the pink smoke of a human corpse
Stockpiles
    of agent orange agent blue agent white acids
    burning like the hot hoof of a race horse on
        the tongue

Look at it
    through the anti-bodies in the body
    through the multiple vaccines belching in the
        veins

    through the cross-infection of viruses
        stockpiled
        in the mouth

    through the benzine vapors shooting
        into the muscles of the
        stars
    through the gaseous bowels of military
        fantasies
    through the white radiation of delirious
        dreams

Look
    this stockpile marries that stockpile
    to mix and release a double stockpile of
        fissions

exploding
    into the shadows of disappearing space
Global incapacitations
Zero

      and boom
This is the nuclear bleach of reality
the inflated thigh of edema
the filthy dampness in the scientific pants
      of a peace prize
the final stockpile of flesh dancing in
the terrible whooping cough of the wind
And even if you think you have a shelter
that can survive this stockpiling
      of communal graves
      tell me

Where are you going
with the sucked liver of mustard flint
the split breath of hydrogen fumes
the navel pit of invisible clams
the biological lung of human fleas
the carcinogenic bladder of sponges
lips made of keloid scars
poems in the numb section of the chromosomes
    Just where do you think you're going
      with that stockpile of
      contaminated stink

Listen
When I think of the tactical missiles plunging
    into the rancid goiters of the sun
The artillery shells of wiretapping snakes hissing and
        vomiting
    into the depths of a colorless sky

The accumulation of fried phosphoric pus graffittied
    on the fragile fierceness of the moon
The pestering warheads of death-wings stockpiling
            feathers upon feathers
                in the brain

And the mass media's larval of lies stockpiled
                in the plasma of the ears

And the stockpiling of foreign sap in the fluxes
        of the blood

And the stockpiling of shattered spines
            in chromium suits
                under
                    polyurethane
                        sheets

    I look at this stockpiling
at this rotting vegetation
and I make myself understand the target
That's why I say I'm into life
        preservation of life now
        revolutionary change now
before the choking
        before the panic
            before the penetration
                    of apathy
                        rises up
                    and spits fire
                into the toxic tears
                    of this stockpile

They Came Again In 1970 in 1980

You didn't send for them
but in the name of god and progress
they came again
Missionaries and scientists arriving
with television sets and microwave ovens
Military advisors landing
with a party of born-again puritans
Bible societies blowing in
with a battery of translators
Bankers coming with loans
with indian-head nickels
Bulldozers entering the undergrowth
from two points in the river
Death exchanging drinks
at the first whiff of petroleum
And in the name of god & progress &
stuffed pockets
after so much torture
& so many invasions in the blood
your veins   are
air strips for
multi-national corporations
Your native sweat is
aviation fuel for
drilling rigs
Your compound is like
a French Devil's Island
And when the eagle flies through
the Amazon rain forest on friday
everything falls into
the pulp of the ferment of your lips
to kiss the landscape goodbye

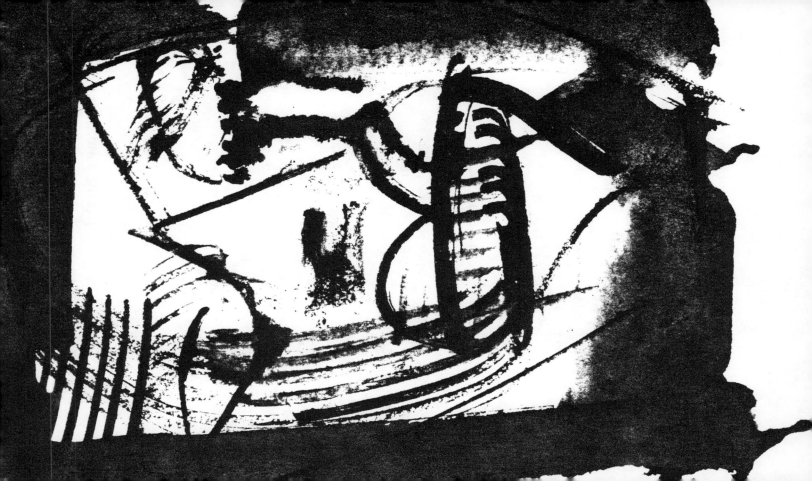

Acceptance Speech

And now to overcome what ?
The secretary's face
The publisher's glasses
Two intellectuals winking to
      each other across the table

A vibration of tv voices
Spectators covered with ball point pens
Pigeons waiting for Amtrak trains
Impulses sent to slash the belly
    carve out the navel
    tear down the day
    plunge into the midnight dump of dead
               chickens
                  to overcome what?

Frivolous gestures of a woman so unnaturally bloated
i'm exhausted
Dying laugh of a man so rotten in the eyes
i hide on the first bus leaving
Stammering dirge of a child so active with fear
i tremble without trembling
exist without existing
overcome without overthrowing
and for that
i'm supposed to thank the producer for
               making it possible
Thank some god for making it happen
Thank my sore butt for thanking you in
the combat tooth of every missing word doing
    time on this rag of discharge reflecting
            back into repression
       back into sexual crust of
          dazzling pigs

to say thanks for filth of rocket sweat in the vulva
Thanks for nostril feathers of metallic boogers in
blood
Thanks for rectum of imperialist flames in shit
Thanks for glow of agent orange pus in orbit
Thanks for the shivering hole of pink foam on fire
Thanks no thanks
   and don't touch it
         ass in front of pain
              don't
                touch it.

Complicity

Who likes to glitter
Who likes to smell blood
Who likes to be real imperialistic
real corrupt

Trade all the gold for a mercedes-benz
Trade all the oil for a peugeot
Trade all the uranium for a rolls royce
Trade all the peanuts for a villa above the Riviera
Trade all the cocoa for a ski lodge in Grenoble
Trade all the traditional art for a case of champagne
Trade all the cobalt for a swiss bank account
Who will buy the outmoded mold
Who will buy the outdated rust
Who will make a billion dollar deal
to store radioactive waste
Who likes to glitter
Who likes to smell blood
Who likes to be real imperialistic
real corrupt

Plain Truth

They say
jab the pencils
in your tongue
Smash windows
Scream
Holler
Tear up the room
Knock down the books
Hold your mouth open with
a stick
Roll over in a rage
Push your private pain
into a collective sadness &
explode
They want you
to hate yourself
in the fly
of their masturbating teeth
Electrocute yourself
in dryness
of their syntax
Suck
their national standard
of
dead metrical feet
and free-base into
refugee camp
of a make-believe
think-tank
They say
walk with
depressive effects

of
a
toxic
cloud
in
your
skull

Keep that
vaginal
aerosol spray
hissing in
the pussy
Store that
contaminated
fetus
of dioxin in
the womb
line those lungs
with the snowflakes
of asbestos
and nuke up to see
the glory
of the coming
of the lord
They want you
to be product
consumer
and public authority
all together in one package
without choice
without change
without a human transforming action
Just enter
emulate & exit

Just puke in
pay off
punk out
and
as soon as you receive
the triple internal illumination
of yourself
as a lunatic
just know
it's a direct hit
in
the
head

In a Stream Of Ink
(For the Print Making Workshop)

So many elbows on the bandstand
　　so many ideologies grafted together
So many memories co-existing
　　so many extensions breaking off
So many scuffles redefined
　　so many secretions interlacing
So many whistles hidden in the flesh
　　so many exaggerated organs on the horizon
So many tongue tampering strategies on the
　　toothbrush
　　so many questions bleeding between dentures
So many uncontrollable punches on the circuit
　　so many edges
So many fringes
　　so many zones
So many flashpoints plunging
　　into the rhythm of the moment

　　　　of so much diversity

that even the finest cloth ever stuffed
into the last tremor of a corpse
can become the rarest vein in the eyeball of
compression
and robot mucus on the sex pulse of nostalgia
can turn into a nuclear warhead of hot semen
and steel dust on the ass of a common pimp
can become a presidential pompadour of acid rain
and the strongest teeth in the grin of humiliation
can become the toothless gums of a fuchsia volcano

And anything and everything is possible
in this collection of umbilical sweat

bursting forth like a mound of a thousand palm
leaves
waving into the space of the night of assaulted bones
Shapes accumulating like ancestors
in the purple velveteen shadow of leather lungs
A ceremony of rakes and rollers crosshatching
into a gel of artificial light
      Clusters
            Patterns
                  Infiltrations

The weight of five overlapping facial configurations
split and glued onto a spleen of lingering odors
Textures   Contours   Colors   Juxtapositions
Half lip   half eye   half day   half tones baptising
in the turquoise darkness of a train serenade
And
in the center of another slab of epidemic wax
a release   a transfer   an accusation   landscapes
a corrosion of marks
head units and gyrating limbs parading
in a stream of black ink
      Elevations
            Stilts

A promenading surface of erotic strokes
Rebellions carried on the felt tip of an evening sunset
Images slashing between the language of reality
and the language of art
Climbing in and out of sensations
in and out of distortions
in and out of the static of chartreuse lightning
With flint and graphite and soot and the knife
grinders grinding into a paint of pink
      champagne

With smoke and stone and grease and the
magnification
    of multiple grooves pressed on a generation of
profiles
With bleach and dye and hemp and the metallic
inflammation
    in eyeslit of a sub-zero bump
With volume and theme and
    the spinning suction cup of Yucatan flames
With flag and map and
    dialogical coagulations on mute of a frozen
plate
With lines
    contracting expanding going deeper
        into the damp sound of the paper
    curving crossing shifting slicing
        into the quiver of a human impulse
    coiling zig-zagging swirling
        into the bite of the process
    pushing piercing swinging from inner
        limitations into outer limits of space
        eliminations

And it's a collographic jungle of cuts
A photographic blister of red dots
Deformed *cabezas* that are secret wells
Mouth murals of flashing metals
A codex of hidden structures
A refuge for absurd feelings
Gouges
    Terrains
Bodies in relief
Bodies absorbed in copper
Bodies subdivided into bodies
    Attitudes

Definitions

Dreams

stretching through a labyrinth of shades
Everything intensifying in this
charcoal sandstorming desert

The buzz in the ear
The blow torch blow of barracuda breath
Barbwire posing on a mask of zinc windows
Apprehensions   Footprints   Invasions
The stench of withdrawal and regeneration
A convulsion of currents   A conduit of
confabulations

Exhaust pipe of lavender flowers

Impressions

from coins   from keys   from anthills
from fifty-five polluted singing winds in a
stream of

so many calculations
    So many conjunctions
so many uninhibited gestures
    So many toxic runoffs
so many self-inflicted etchings
    So many reef devastations
so many identification stones smoking
    So many tilted forms feathered
so many insertions inserted
    So many conceptions communicated
so many enclosures
    So many events
so many blunted instruments scraping
    into the rhythm of the moment
        of so much diversity

When I Look At Wilfredo Lam's Paintings

They have breasts shaped
like papayas like grapefruits like
spades & shovels & picks & mangos

They erupt
and swirl into baby tornados
They mutate and chalk into
burnt out bulbs of
decorated pus in paint

They merge and melt into other forms
Swallow themselves and gush forward

They connect their sockets
to spermatic strings
of dried centipedes
moving in half steps toward
center of the darkness of the dot
to become ancestral shadows
saturated between Damballah's tattooed toes
and Oya's fishhook fingers
between Ogun's rust colored neck
and Oshun's wine coated tongue
between Shango's red leaves matted to
tiny pyramid teeth of a barking sorcerer
and Yemaya's silver-rimmed eyelids expanding
and contracting into a cyclonic breeze of
double-headed bats

They burn up the brushes
with raffia swishing and shooting from
buttocks of vibrating nostrils

with knee-caps swelling on stilts of
bowlegged nails
with grinning horses galloping from
navels of frying fat
with purple stems of cane protruding from
green lips of machetes
with zigzagging flamingos fluctuating on
the roof tops of Matanzas

They billow and overlap in broaches of
charcoal spittle
They cross and dissolve into
a fleet of orange blotted organs
They have their bull horns
their yellow snake arrows
their triangular forest skulls
their blood vessels sprouting from daggers
their upsidedown faces in pelvises rotating
and perforating in spider specked sex of the gouache

I and I
(for Michael Smith)

We had a nice time together
traveling   laughing   eating   drinking
reading our poetry
in jam sessions

       carving up rhythms
       carving up syllables
       carving up time
              I and I

Now they say
you be dead in your dreads Michael
Stoned to death
by some treacherous Black brothers
in your own country
           of Jamaica

And hey
You were worried about the White Man
about not receiving berries from
grave of a Russian writer
about the theft of black talk
in mouth of a punk rocker
about the customs officer
who tried to block your re-entry
             into Paris

Yeah man
It must've been
a mean verbal extension
           of the dozens
that you laid
on those reactionary elite politicians
to cause such a tremor of hate
to flare off

and become fanatical in them
and in their followers
who had already suffered
from a loss of consciousness
    a loss of purpose
        a loss of self

And I can just see you
tearing the night up
with the intensity of your stare-down
tearing it up
with your blistering cadre
        of rebellious rhymes
        And it is what it is
from this word to that word
from that event to this event
from here to there to where
men with occupations emphasizing the
                precisions of
                    death
    rather than the precisions in life come
    out through the bacteria of walls
not to hear the sound of your reggae sound
not to see you smile your natural smile
not to understand the concept of your conceptual
                ways of dealing
but to familiarize themselves with the functions
of shutting off voices shutting out faces
        shutting out names
And it is what it is
    in front of that kind of energy of confusion
    that mysticism of madness
    that homicidal hipness which

you yourself alone tried to penetrate as
the build up between dominance and resistance
                                          threw down
                                          at full cry
And the cross-road-smells collided and flashed back
to the day you demanded to be treated like a human
being
back to the day you entered the ritual compound to
be
an African saluting Africa
back to the day you declared yourself a poet with
a message from the people enslaved in poverty
back to the day you called for justice
That was the day you became a threat to
the life style of the bourgeois class of beggars
                                          in Babylon

That was when they decided
you were an insane dangerous infant   opposed
to their neo-colonial out-house mentality
That was when they vowed to
blow away the Stagolee in your mental fire
To put paraquat in your holy weed
to turn the erotic vitality of stone
into signifying stones
into tribal stones
into a stigma of stones
against your complexion of Blackness
against your language of revolt
against your spiritual defiance
against the slash of your limping
                     leg of steel
And it was a rain of boulders shooting
in and out of your skull
                     like bombs

A burst of red lava in the air
A greenish bolt of lighting
      in the center of the unity of space
Your baby teeth going back into the earth
back into the hearts of the poets
who break open their lines to
sing your wolfing wolof words
straight through the pathological
invasions of the hour
straight through the emergency wards
of agitated officials
straight through the bull's-eye of the cyclone

Solomon Mahlangu
Freedom Fighter From Mamelodi

They tried to force Solomon Mahlangu
  to swallow their shitball ideology of apartheid
    Tried to make him a burning carrier
      of their bantustan madness
Tried to contaminate him
  with their infectious passbook plague
    They wanted him to be
      a castrated lopsided afrikaans speaking scavenger
      a drunk wornout mimicking collector of fascist
culture
  a sticky unborn unconceived spot on the reservation
But he went outside of their wants
  outside of their needs
  and built up a defense system
    against the secretion of insanity and fear
Vaccinated himself
  against the inflamed mucus
  of Pessimistic White Inept
  Reactionary Arrogantitus Syndrome (PWIRAS)
    Became immune
      to the compounds used to separate people
    Sprinkled his body
    with the blood of other revolutionary warriors
And by the time his fist flew up
  and his heart shot forward
    like ten king cobras
      in the pre-dawn spit of April
        he had already
          gone beyond the realities of life

Push Back the Catastrophes

I don't want a drought to feed on itself
through the tattooed holes in my belly
I don't want a spectacular desert of
charred stems & rabbit hairs
in my throat of accumulated matter
I don't want to burn and cut through the forest
like a greedy mercenary drilling into
the sugar cane of the bones

Push back the advancing sands
the polluted sewage
the dust demons   the dying timber
the upper atmosphere of nitrogen
push back the catastrophes

Enough of the missiles
the submarines
the aircraft carriers
the biological weapons
No more sickness   sadness   poverty
exploitation   destabilization
illiteracy and bombing
Let's move toward peace
toward equality and justice
that's what I want

To breathe clean air
to drink pure water to plant new crops
to soak up the rain to wash off the stink
to hold this body and soul together in peace
that's it
Push back the catastrophes

Everything is Wonderful

Under the urination of astronauts
and the ejaculation of polluted sparrows
and the evacuation of acid brain matter
everything is wonderful
except for the invasion and occupation
of Grenada
except for the avalanche of blood coagulating
in El Salvador
except for the brutal apartheid system
raging in South Africa
except for the threat of intervention
in Nicaragua
except for the war of repression
in Namibia
except for Pinochet creaming again
this very day
from the killing floor of Allende and Neruda
except for that
and the torrential rainfall
of cluster bombs falling in Beirut
everything is everything
wonderful and wonderful

Expenditures
Economic Love Song 1

MILITARY SPENDING HUGE PROFITS & DEATH

MILITARY SPENDING HUGE PROFITS & DESTRUCTION

MILITARY SPENDING HUGE PROFITS & DEATH

MILITARY SPENDING HUGE PROFITS & DESTRUCTION

MILITARY SPENDING HUGE PROFITS & DEATH

MILITARY SPENDING HUGE PROFITS & DESTRUCTION

MILITARY SPENDING HUGE PROFITS & DEATH

MILITARY SPENDING HUGE PROFITS & DESTRUCTION

MILITARY SPENDING HUGE PROFITS & DEATH

MILITARY SPENDING HUGE PROFITS & DESTRUCTION

MILITARY SPENDING HUGE PROFITS & DEATH

MILITARY SPENDING HUGE PROFITS & DESTRUCTION

MILITARY SPENDING HUGE PROFITS & DEATH

MILITARY SPENDING HUGE PROFITS & DESTRUCTION

MILITARY SPENDING HUGE PROFITS & DEATH

MILITARY SPENDING HUGE PROFITS & DESTRUCTION

MILITARY SPENDING HUGE PROFITS & DEATH

MILITARY SPENDING HUGE PROFITS & DESTRUCTION

MILITARY SPENDING HUGE PROFITS & DEATH

MILITARY SPENDING HUGE PROFITS & DESTRUCTION

MILITARY SPENDING HUGE PROFITS & DESTRUCTION

MILITARY SPENDING HUGE PROFITS & DEATH

MILITARY SPENDING HUGE PROFITS & DESTRUCTION

MILITARY SPENDING HUGE PROFITS & DEATH

Tell Me

Tell me that the plutonium sludge
in your corroded torso is all a dream

Tell me that your penis bone is not erupting
with the stench of dead ants
that your navel is not the dump site
                of contaminated pus
that the spillage from your hard ass
is not a fallout of radioactive waste
Tell me it's a lie
Tell me it's a joke

Tell me that you don't have to fuck yourself on
the reactor core of an intense meltdown
                to show your importance
Tell me that you have no desire
to be the first one to fuck
      into the fission of a fusion
         of a fucking holocaust

Tell me i'm hallucinating
Tell me i'm fantasizing
Tell me i'm delirious
Tell me you know peace is better than war
that total decolonization is better than war
that the elimination of hunger is better than war
that the moon merging into the shadow of the earth
              is better than war

That night moving into day
and day moving   back into night is better than war
That the sound of the human voice in its calmness
in its shrillness

in its monumental invention of pitches
                    is better than war

that the arrival of rain
the smell of something familiar
the blood circulating in your legs
the visitation of the sun
the conjunction of rivers
the vexation of your special nerve and
hope rising from the soul of your nose
                    is better than war

Tell me that the tonnage of nuclear sweat
in your prostrate gland is all a mistake
tell me that your vagina
        will not be
                a bursting silo of blue flames
that your chest
        will not be
                an infested swamp of vomiting mosquitos

Tell me it's a mirage
Tell me it's absurd
Tell me you really have no intention of being
a homeless   nameless   sexless piece of shit
                somewhere over the rainbow

Tell me that you have no need to get high
                off the fumes of a neutron bomb
Tell me that you're not going to peel off your skin
and be a psychedelic corpse in the holy water of
                        patriotic slobber

Tell me it's ridiculous
Tell me it's ludicrous

But don't tell me that you think you're immune
        because there is no immunity

No immunity to the hydrogen dust
    moving like a cloud
        of a hundred trillion infuriated rhinos
No immunity to the fireball smoker
        of abdominal organs
No immunity to the fetishes wrapped
            in uranium crates
No immunity to the downwind flames
            of invisible radiation

No immunity
    and you know it
        i know it
            the computer knows it
                everybody knows it

So tell me that you're going to pull away
    from the corrupt gluttonous controllers of profit
Tear open the condescending attitudes
                full of green ashes
Separate yourself from the solitude of stagnation
Don't tell me that you want to sink into the stink
                    of exotic weapons
Don't tell me that you want to quiver into the heat
                of missile repulsion
Don't tell me that you want to disappear
            into the pessimistic past
            of your own self-interest

Tell me i'm dreaming
Tell me i'm hallucinating
Tell me i'm fantasizing
Tell me it's unthinkable
Tell me it's unrealistic
Tell me it's all in my imagination
Tell me you never heard of such a thing

Tell me it's a misunderstanding
Tell me it's not a human need
Tell me it's a crock of shit
Tell me it's propaganda
Tell me you really intend to go forward
Tell me
Tell me
Tell me

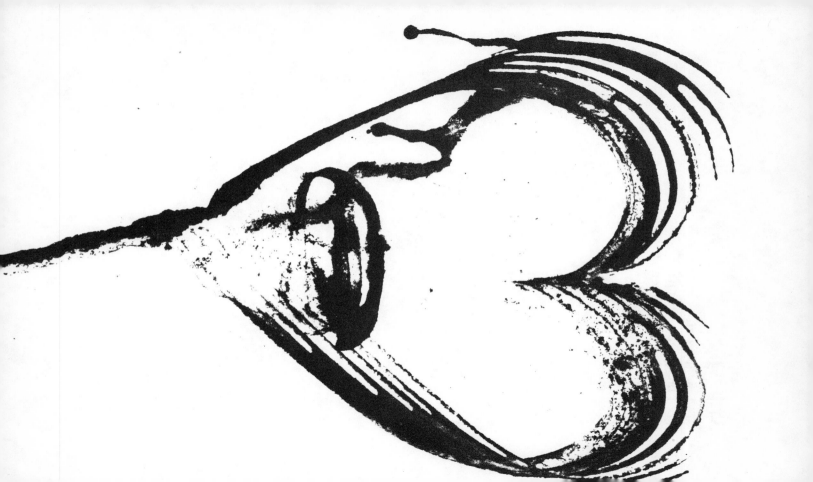

Glossary

For the Poets:
kai kai   a homemade gin in Nigeria
Akpetesie   a homemade gin in Ghana
Nsukka   a city in Eastern Nigeria
Damballah   the god of fertility in Haiti
skokian   a homemade gin in South Africa
Basuto   a group of people in Lesotho

Rose Solitude:
Shango   Yoruba god of thunder in Nigeria
Erzulie   a sea goddess in Haiti

Firespitters:
Lagos   a capital city of Nigeria
Nupe   a group of people in Nigeria

The Red Pepper Poet:
zydeco   traditional form of Black music in Louisiana
ibeji   twins
Boni   a group of people in French Guiana

Rape:
Inez Garcia, Joanne Little   Rape victims in the
1970s

I See Chano Pozo:
Atamo   various Africa drums
Mpebi
Donno
Obonu
Atumpan
Mpintintoa
Ntenga

Siky Akkua
Bata
Fontomfrom
Lucumi   a religious cult in Cuba
Abakwa   secret society cult in Cuba

When I Look At Wilfredo Lam's Paintings:

Damballah   the god of fertility in Haiti
Oya   goddess of the river Niger in Nigeria
Ogun   Yoruba god of iron and war in Nigeria
Oshun   goddess of the river Oshun
Shango   Yoruba god of thunder
Yemaya   goddess of the sea in Cuba

Jayne Cortez was born in Arizona, grew up in California and is currently living in New York City. Her poetry has been published in many journals, magazines, and anthologies including Confirmation, New Black Voices, Giant Talk, Free Spirits, Presence Africaine and the Unesco Courier. She is the author of five books of poetry and three recordings. Her latest book is *Firespitter* and her recording of poetry *There It Is* was released in 1982. She has lectured and read her poetry alone and with music throughout the United States, West Africa, Europe and the Caribbean.